HEY! I'm Reading!

A how-to-read book for beginners

by Betty Miles

illustrated by Sylvie Wickstrom

 Alfred A. Knopf • New York

For my favorite readers—
Margaret, Sophie, and Katie

Sesame Street logo used by permission of
Children's Television Workshop

THIS IS A BORZOI BOOK PUBLISHED BY ALFRED A. KNOPF, INC.

Text copyright © 1995 by Betty Miles
Illustrations © 1995 by Sylvie Wickstrom
All rights reserved under International and Pan-American Copyright Conventions.
Published in the United States of America by Alfred A. Knopf, Inc., New York, and
simultaneously in Canada by Random House of Canada Limited, Toronto.
Distributed by Random House, Inc., New York.

Library of Congress Cataloging-in-Publication Data
Hey! I'm Reading!/by Betty Miles
illustrated by Sylvie Wickstrom. p. cm.
ISBN 0-679-85644-7 (trade pbk.) ISBN 0-679-95644-1 (lib. bdg.)
1. Reading (Primary—Juvenile literature.) [1. Reading. 2. Readers.]
I.Wickstrom, Sylvie II. Title.
LB1525.M54 1994 372.41—dc20 93-2588

Manufactured in the United States of America
2 4 6 8 0 9 7 5 3 1

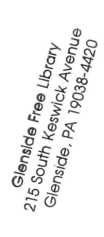

PARTS OF THE BOOK

A Message for New Readers

This is a book for children who are 4, 5, 6, or more years old, who go to school now or will be going soon. That's the time when most people begin to be readers. It's probably when you're beginning to be a reader, too.

You may wonder when you will be able to read anything you want. No one can tell you that exactly. There isn't one special day, like your birthday or the first day of first grade, when you're suddenly supposed to know how. Reading is like growing — it happens slowly, a little bit at a time.

You already know a lot about reading, and you are learning more about it every

day. When you listen to books, read a STOP sign, or write the letters of your name, you are learning about reading. Once you begin to be a reader, you can keep on reading, all the rest of your life.

This book is to help you begin.

Part 1

Some Things You Already Know About Reading

It takes a long time to get ready to read. It takes years!

You've been getting ready all your life, without even thinking about it, just by growing up. You already know a lot about reading right now.

Here are six important things you know:

1. You know that it's good to be able to read!

2. You know that what you read is writing. You see writing wherever you go:

on trucks

and on T-shirts,

on buildings

and on boxes.

You may even see it
in the sky!

Wherever you see it, you know that writing means
something. Reading is figuring out what the writing means.

3. You know that letters are part of writing. You probably know the names of some letters. Maybe you can write some. Maybe you can write the letters in your name.

4. You certainly know how to talk! Talking is good practice for reading.

When you talk, you say words. When you read, you read words.

4

When you were a baby, you only knew a few words.

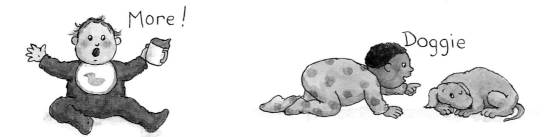

Now you know thousands. You know how they sound and what they mean and how to use them to say what you want.

You know what? Yesterday I went to my grandmother's house, and she has this cute little dog named Queenie, and she let me take Queenie for a walk on a leash, and we went to the park, and then this big dog came over and we thought he was going to chase us, but then Queenie barked so loud he ran away.

By now, you're an expert talker. You already know most of the words you're going to read.

5. You know about books. You know there are different kinds of books,

like fact books

and cookbooks

and storybooks.

You know how to turn the pages of a book.
You may know that the words on a page go from left to right.
You know that when you come to the end of a page, you go

on to the next page.

You know where a book begins

and where it ends.

You know that when you come to the end of a book, you can go back to the beginning and read it again.

6. Here is the most important thing you know about reading: You already know so many of the things that you will read about.

You know about dogs and cats,

rain and umbrellas.

You know about friends.

You know about the moon and the stars,

about spaceships and astronauts.

You know about tying shoes and zipping zippers.

You know how to make wishes

and how to make sandwiches.

You know how it feels to love somebody.

You will read about all of these things!

Are you beginning to be a reader?
Here are 10 questions to help you find out.

1. Are you 4, 5, 6, or more years old?
2. Do you like to talk?
3. Do you like to listen?
4. Can you write your name?
5. Can you already read some words?
6. Can you make up a story to go with these pictures?

7. Can you remember a story from a book?
8. Do you like books?
9. Do you like to learn new things?
10. Do you want to learn how to read?

If you said YES to most of these questions, you are beginning to be a reader now.

Part 2

Some Ways
to Read

When you first begin to read, you probably wonder how people do it. Learning to read seems pretty amazing.

Learning to read *is* amazing. But it's something that almost everyone can do, just as almost everyone can learn how to talk.

Learning to read is like learning to talk: you start slowly, but the more you do it, the easier it gets.

When you want to say something, you don't stop and think about each word you're going to use. You just talk.

After a while, you will read in the same way. You won't have to stop and figure out every word; you'll just read. That's when reading gets really interesting. Then you can read whatever you want.

But at first most new readers do have to figure out the words.

Luckily, there are lots of ways to do this. You can try one way and then another. Any way that helps you to read is good. This part of the book tells you about six different ways.

1. Getting Help from Pictures

Most new readers are good at looking at pictures. What you see in a picture can help you figure out the words that go with it.

If you see this picture on a can at the grocery store, you probably have a good idea of what the word says:

You can probably figure out the words on these cans of paint:

and on these crayons:

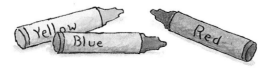

This picture helps you read the name of the book.

And this picture helps you to read what the mother is saying.

Pictures often help you to read. Looking carefully at pictures is a good way to begin.

2. Remembering

There will always be some words that you can read as soon as you see them, because you remember them. That's probably the way you read your name.

You don't need a picture of yourself to help you read your name! You just know it when you see it, because you've seen it so many times before. You read it without thinking about it. You remember the whole word.

All readers remember words that way. Older readers can remember hundreds — even thousands — of words.

New readers begin to remember words as soon as they begin to read, and the list of words they know grows bigger every day.

People remember words for different reasons.

If you live on Pine Tree Road, you can probably read your street sign by sight.

If you watch TV, you may remember these words very well.

If you go to the Piggly Wiggly supermarket every day, you can probably read its name because you remember it.

Sometimes the shape of a word helps you to remember. You may remember

hippopotamus

because it's sort of big and bumpy, like the animal.

If you live in the state of Mississippi, you probably remember its long name.

Sometimes short words are harder to remember. There are so many of them!

Here are three little words you will often see when you read:

a   and   the

If you can remember them, you won't have to figure them out each time you see them.

Once upon a time,
a pig, a duck, and
a horse set out to see
the world. The duck rode
on the horse's back, and
the pig trotted along
beside them.

The word **a** is easy to remember, because it's just one letter. Here it is with some other words:

a dinosaur

a hippopotamus

a cat

a dog

A girl and **a** boy are friends.

A word you say a lot is **and.** You will see it a lot when you read, too.

I like peas **and** lettuce **and** tomatoes. **And** watermelon, too!

PEAS

LETTUCE

TOMATOES

WATERMELON

You often say the word **the**, and you will often see it when you read.

The girl hit **the** ball over **the** wall. Yay!

The more you read, the better you will remember these three little words:

a   **and**   **the**

Reading gets easier when you remember words. You don't have to figure them out each time. You just see them and read them.

But you can't remember every word you see. You need other ways to help you read.

A B C D E F G H I J K L M

a b c d e f g h i j k l m

3. Sounding Out the Letters

Every word in this book is made out of letters from a list called the alphabet.

There are 26 letters in the alphabet. There are two ways to write each one — in capital letters, **A B C**, and in lowercase letters, **a b c**.

Each letter of the alphabet has a name, like **M,** and a sound, like the sound at the beginning of **milk** or **monkey.**

NOPQRSTUVWXYZ

nopqrstuvwxyz

When you say the name of the letter **I**, you are reading a whole word!

If you say the name of the letter **O**, and then the name of this one, **K,** you have said another word: **OK.** Can you read it?

23

If you know the names of the letters **T** and **V**, you can read this: **TV**.

Many new readers like to find words that begin with the same first letter as their names.

If your name is **Sam** or **Sara** or **Sophie** or **Sylvie** or **Susan** or **Sula** or **Sonny** or **Saul**, you may like to look for words that begin with an **S.**

You can hear the sound of the letter **s** at the beginning of lots of words:

snake

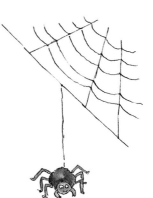

spider

star

strawberry

seesaw

school

Even if your name doesn't start with **S**, you may know that letter now.

Sounding out the first letter helps you begin to say these words:

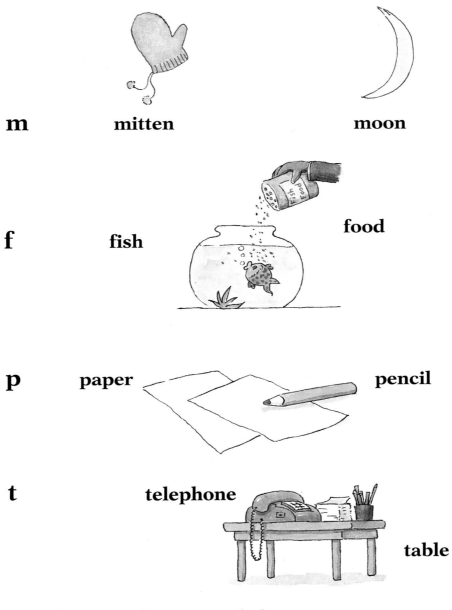

m   **mitten**   **moon**

f   **fish**   **food**

p   **paper**   **pencil**

t   **telephone**

                        table

Of course, the pictures help, too.

c   **cat**   **can**

Sometimes, just one new letter sound can make a whole new word.

Say **f** with **at,** and you hear **fat.**

Say **c** with **at,** and you hear **cat.**

Say **s** with **at,** and you hear **sat.**

Say **h** with **at,** and you hear **hat.**

The **fat cat sat** on the **hat.**

Listen to the sounds of the first letters in these words:

can   **man**   **pan**

Can a **man** sit in a **pan?**

Listening to letter sounds can help you to read. The more you read, the more you will learn about letter sounds.

But sounding out won't always work, because letters don't always sound the way you think they will.

Some letters have more than one sound. And in some words, a letter may not make any sound at all!

Knock, knock!
Knock, knock, knock!

If somebody knocks on the door in a story you're reading, you don't say the word like this: **k-nock, k-nock!**

You don't say the **k** at all. You read the word as if the letter weren't there.

The fact is that some words are written in really ridiculous ways! When you begin to read, you will find some words that are hard to sound out. But as you go on reading, you will learn to read the hard words, too.

4. Expecting What Comes Next

Some words just seem to go together. When you hear one, you expect the other one. When you read one, you expect the other one. That helps you to read it.

in and **out**

up and **down**

on and **off**

ice cream and **cake**

night and **day**

peanut butter and **jelly**

29

Sometimes when you talk, you say the same words over and over.

And sometimes when you read, you see the same words over and over, too. You begin to expect them. That helps you to read them. Like this:

around and around and around

When you read the words of a song, you begin to expect some words to come around again.

Go in and out the window,
Go in and out the window,
Go in and out the window
As we have done before.

Expecting what comes next is part of reading. Do you know the song about Old MacDonald?

Old MacDonald had a farm
E I, E I, O.
And on this farm he had a pig
E I, E I, O.
With an oink, oink here,
And an **oink, oink** there,
Here an **oink,** there an **oink,**
Everywhere an **oink, oink—**
Old MacDonald had a farm
E I, E I, O.

OINK
OINK

Poems often have words that rhyme, like **day** and **play**.
Sometimes you can guess the rhyming word. You expect it to
come.

Rain, rain, go away,
Come again some other day.
All the children want to **play**.

It's raining,
It's pouring.
The old man is **snoring**.

When you expect words to come along, reading them is easier.

One potato,
Two **potato,**
Three **potato,** four.
Five **potato,**
Six **potato,**
Seven **potato, more!**

I scream,
You **scream,**
We all **scream**
For **ice cream!**

5. Writing

A very good way to learn to read words is to write them yourself.

You can probably write a few words already. When you write the letters of words, you notice how they look and how they sound together. You know what you're saying, because you're writing it.

Every time you write a word, you are reading it.

Putting the letters together to make words is called spelling. If you don't know how to spell a word, you can ask someone to help you. Or you can try to spell it yourself, the way it sounds to you. People can probably read what you write. Or you can read it to them.

Suppose you want to write **I love you.**

You know how to write the first word—it's just one letter: **I.**

You may not know how to spell **love.** Try it, anyway.

If you write **luv** or **lv,** someone will be able read it.

Even if you just draw a  people will know what you mean.

You may not know how to spell **you** but you probably know the name of the letter **u,** which sounds just like the word. So you could just write **u.**

Here are four different ways to write **I love you:**

I love you is really the right way. But however you write it, someone will be very glad to read it!

6. Making Sense

When you talk, you try to make sense to the person you're talking to.

When you read, what you're reading needs to make sense to you. You have to understand it.

One way to find out if you're reading something right is to see if it makes sense to you.

If something you're reading doesn't make sense, you may want to read it again. Ask yourself: Does this sound right? Does it make sense?

I am a **grill.**
I am a **girl.**

Hey, **pots!**
Hey, **stop!**

Put this sandwich in a **bug.**
Put this sandwich in a **bag.**

Put the garbage in the **cap.**
Put the garbage in the **can.**

I live in **hippopotamus.**
I live in **Mississippi.**

If what you read makes sense to you, you're probably reading it right.

Six Ways to Read

1. **Getting help from pictures.** A picture can help to tell you what the words say.

2. **Remembering.** You remember some words because you see them over and over.

3. **Sounding out the letters.** The sounds of the letters in a word can help you to read it.

4. **Expecting what comes next.** Expecting words to come along makes you ready to read them.

5. **Writing.** Writing words is good practice for reading them.

6. **Making sense.** If what you read makes sense to you, you're probably reading it right.

Of course, you don't know everything about reading yet. You will learn more every day, like every other reader. Each time you read something, you learn more about reading.

The rest of the pages in this book are for you to read by yourself or with somebody else. You may not be able to read everything the first time. That's OK. You are just beginning to read now. Soon you will be able to read lots of pages in lots of books.

Have fun reading!

Part 3

20 Pages for You to Read Yourself

Hello? Hello!

Happy Birthday

The Mad Story

You did!

I did not!

Yes, you did!

No, I didn't!

Did!

Didn't!

Oh, yes, you did!

No, I did not!

At the Store

43

Knock, Knock!

Bad News, Good News

It's raining.

But I have an umbrella!

Oops! Ice cream on my T-shirt.

But I can wash it off!

My T-shirt is too small.

But I can give it to my sister!

My dog is lost.

Woof!

But I found him!

45

An Alphabet of Names

The Long Good-bye

See you later, Alligator.

See you later, Alligator!

See you LATER, Alligator!

SEE YOU LATER, ALLIGATOR!

GOOD-BYE!

OH, NO!

OH, YES!

See you later, Hippopotamus!

The Two Roberts

Robert A. is six. So is Robert B.

Robert A. is in first grade. So is Robert B.

Robert A. loves to read. So does Robert B.

Robert A. likes to paint. So does Robert B.

Robert A. loves spaghetti. Robert B. loves pizza.

Robert A. and Robert B. like to climb
on the jungle gym.

Robert A. and Robert B. climb up
up, up, to the top of the jungle gym.
"Look at me!" says Robert A.
"Look at me!" says Robert B.
"Hey! Look at us!" they say.

Robert A. and Robert B. are
very good friends.

Halloween

Library Time

The Socks in the Wash

The socks in the wash
Go around and around,
Around and around and around.
One sock, two socks,
Red socks, blue socks.
Yellow socks, green socks,
Dirty socks, clean socks!
The socks in the wash
Go around and around,
Around and around and around.

The Door at the Store

I used to get hit by the door
That opens itself at the store.
I used to begin
To push OUT
To go IN,
But I never do that anymore.
I can read!

Some Puzzles 4 U

The Loose Tooth

wiggle *wiggle* *wiggle* *wiggle*

My tooth is loose!

wiggle *wiggle* *wiggle* *wiggle*

Will it come out?

wiggle *wiggle* *wiggle* *wiggle*

It's so loose!

wiggle *wiggle* *wiggle*

It's almost out!

wiggle *wiggle*

Hey! It came out!

HEY, LOOK!

MY TOOTH CAME OUT!

Time for School

In School

57

Love Story

The End

That's all there is.
There isn't any more.
But if you can read,
You can read it again—
From the beginning
All
    the
        way
           to
              THE END!

BETTY MILES has taught kindergarten children and graduate students, led workshops with parents, teachers, and librarians, and talked about books and reading with children in schools around the country. She was an Associate Editor of the first Bank Street Readers and is the author of 25 books for young readers, including *Save the Earth: An Action Handbook for Kids*.